SONNETS OF LOUISE LABÉ

Translated by ALTA LIND COOK

THE love sonnets of Louise Labé of Lyons and the gilded legend of her life in the early years of the French Renaissance have appealed to the imagination of four centuries.

Printed here beside the text of the 1556 edition, the translations of the sonnets by Alta Lind Cook follow closely the original version and admirably retain its sweep and movement, its simplicity and melody. The rhyme scheme of the Petrarchan sonnet has been preserved with variations corresponding to those of the French. With the poems, the translator presents a sketch of the circumstances and background of this unique literary figure of the Sixteenth Century, known in France and outside of France as *La Belle Cordière.*

These translations by Alta Lind Cook are fine poetry; in English as in French the reader finds "present reality in their hope and their despair, their independence and their impertinence, their tears and their sparkle." *(From the Preface.)*

SONNETS

OF

LOUISE LABÉ

« *LA BELLE CORDIÈRE* »

*

Translated into English Verse by
ALTA LIND COOK

TORONTO
UNIVERSITY OF TORONTO PRESS
1950

Copyright, Canada, 1950
University of Toronto Press
Reprinted in paperback 2015
London: Geoffrey Cumberlege
Oxford University Press
ISBN 978-1-4426-3932-4 (paper)

PREFACE

T H E sonnets of Louise Labé, published in 1555, make one of those human documents which help to bridge the distances of time and space. There is a present reality in their hope and their despair, their independence and their impertinence, their tears and their sparkle. They tell a deeply personal story. And so they have survived.

Translations in recent times bear witness to interest outside of France: the sonnets were translated in 1917 into German by Rainer Maria Rilke (Leipzig); in 1924 into German by Sophie Jacot des Combes (Zurich); in 1924 into Dutch by P. C. Boutens (Maastricht); in 1947 into English by Frederic Prokosch (New York).

This translation has been in preparation for several years, having been undertaken first for the purpose of illustrating a public lecture given at Victoria College in the University of Toronto. It is offered here as an attempt at transposition into English of the original French with its simplicity and its melody. The rhyme scheme of the Petrarchan sonnet has been preserved with variations in the tercets following those of the corresponding French.

The opportunity is taken at this time to express appreciation of the friendly assistance given to the writer in her personal discovery of sixteenth-century Lyons, with thanks to Monsieur Jean Tricou particularly; to Monsieur Magnin of the Library of the City of Lyons, and to Monsieur Dalbanne of the Guadagne Museum; also to Monsieur and Madame Chalandon of Parcieu for the generous hospitality of their beautiful home, which is known as *La Grange Blanche,* and which is the house bought by Louise Labé in 1557.

For critical reading of the manuscript, thanks are due to Professor Donald M. Frame of Columbia University, and to Professor Robert D. C. Finch of University College, University of Toronto.

A. L. C.

Toronto
February, 1950

The text of the poems follows the 1556 edition published by Jean de Tournes: "Euvres de Louïse Labé Lionnoize. Revues & corrigees par ladite Dame." For the convenience of the modern reader, the present-day forms, "s," "u," and "j," have been used.

The title-page decorations are also derived from the 1556 edition.

LOUISE LABE OF LYONS

F O U R centuries ago, on the illustrated map of the City of Lyons completed in 1553, there appeared a new street name, *la rue de la Belle Cordière,* the Street of the Beautiful Wife of the Ropemaker.

The cordier or ropemaker was the middle-aged Ennemond Perrin. His beautiful wife was Louise Labé, known in all Lyons and beyond not only for her beauty but for her accomplishments. She was skilled in military exercises and games as her brothers were, and rode with such daring that friends, in fun and admiration, called her *Capitaine Loys.* She was renowned for her playing of that difficult instrument, the lute, and for her singing. She was a woman of letters, leaving a volume published by Jean de Tournes in 1555 which contained a Dedicatory Epistle, a play, three elegies, twenty-four sonnets, and poems written in her honour by some of the most distinguished men of her time. In her library were to be found books in Spanish, Italian, and Latin as well as French. Contemporary opinion was divided as to her virtue and a literary debate on the subject has continued for four hundred years.

Louise Labé was born in 1520 or before, early in the reign of Francis I. She was the daughter by a second marriage of Pierre Charly, known by the name of Labé which was traditional in the prosperous ropemaking business which he conducted in *la rue de l'Arbre-Sec.* Pierre Labé could not sign his name to the receipts for loans to the king, preserved in the City Archives; but the loans were substantial. It is a matter for conjecture whether it was he who may have been responsible, in this cosmopolitan city of the early Renaissance, for the remarkable education acquired by his brilliant daughter, an education of mind and body thoroughly Italian in conception.

These were the days when kings brought their courts to Lyons to sojourn for months while they assembled and provisioned their armies, and when the luxuries and freedoms and the New Learning of the Italian Renaissance found their way naturally and easily to this prosperous city which lay on the road south to Rome. Here, as in Italy, women presided at social gatherings which were forerunners of the *salons* of the seventeenth century; and enthusiasm for the new doctrine of Platonism, the cult of the ideal in beauty and friendship, amounted to a religious fervour. In the popular translation of Castiglione's book of manners, *Le Courtisan,* Frenchwomen could read that there is nothing more desirable and fitting for a woman than knowledge. Cardinal Bembo had advised that a little girl should be taught Latin as a crowning grace. And in that book of fun and wisdom recounting the exploits of the giant prince Gargantua, published in Lyons when Louise was fourteen years of age, Rabelais had written that the ladies of Thélème had to be miracles of learning as well as of beauty and elegance, to be fit companions for men.

What circumstances, what ambitions may have inspired the young Louise Labé, daughter of artisans, to acquire the education of a great lady, no one can tell. There are few facts on which to build the story of her youth. It is in her third elegy that she speaks of the studies, the chivalric games and riding, the exercises of mind and body, together with practice in the art of needle-work, which occupied what she calls her *"verd aage,"* her "green age," until, at sixteen, she fell in love. For eight years from that time there is no record, though a legend persists that she rode with the army of the Dauphin to the siege of Perpignan in 1542, and there are references to a soldier, *"un homme de guerre,"* whom she loved. Then when she was twenty-four or twenty-five, a scandalously advanced age for a woman still to be unwed in those days, her father married her to a man twice as old as she, whose modest business was down in that small street near the old Rhône bridge, not far from the hospital where Rabelais saw his patients in the district of Notre Dame de Confort. Before the "privilege" for her book was granted in 1554, Ennemond Perrin died childless, leaving all his property to his wife. In 1555 the book was published by the printing house of Jean de Tournes. It had considerable success, three new editions being printed in 1555, one of them in Rouen. Then in 1557, in her own name, Louise Labé bought a property in the country at Parcieu en Dombes about twenty-five kilometres from the city—a house of quiet dignity which still stands beautifully preserved, looking across wide lawns and down upon a peaceful stretch of fields and trees where the Saône winds lazily.

In 1565, while seriously ill, she made her will at the

home of Thomas Fortin, a Florentine banker resident in Lyons who was her faithful friend for the last eight years of her life. It is a considerate document in which she leaves most of her property to two "well-loved" nephews but remembers to reserve sums to be given in dowry to poor girls of the neighbourhood and to former servants and small tradesmen. In 1566, she died at her home at Parcieu, after what seems to have been a long illness. She was buried at Parcieu, and Thomas Fortin bought a stone to mark her grave. But all traces of grave and stone have disappeared. Her considerable property, at the early death of her nephews, went, as directed by her will, to the Poor Fund of the City of Lyons.

These are the scant facts of the life of Louise Labé. Some sympathetic biographers have given her the place in Lyons society of the day for which her beauty and talents would have fitted her. They have represented her as taking part in the luxurious and colourful spectacles of the time, the masques and mysteries, the *"Entrées Solonnelles,"* those magnificent and gala occasions of civic welcome to eminent visitors. The wealthy bourgeois paid generously and pridefully for such displays as that of the Entry of Henri II and Catharine de Medici in 1548, when the scenario was written by Maurice Scève, illustrious dean of Lyons poets. Louise Labé has been pictured as a pupil of Maurice Scève and a friend of his gifted and charming sisters, and as having a salon of her own down in the district of Notre Dame de Confort. Four hundred years have gilded the legend.

It is certain, however, that some of the most bril-

liant men of letters of that day visited her in her home
and held her in high esteem. Among those who wrote
poems in her praise are Clément Marot, Maurice
Scève, Olivier de Magny, Pontus de Tyard, and
Antoine du Moulin (possibly responsible for one of
the two poems addressed to her in Greek). Of par-
ticular interest is an ode, *A Louise Labé Lionnoise,*
written by Jacques Peletier du Mans, scholar, doctor,
and mathematician, and published in the second
volume of his *Art poétique* (Lyon, 1555). After men-
tion of the lovely *Damoisèles et Dames* of Lyons, he
writes:

Mes j'an è vù sur toutes autres l'une,
Resplandissant comme de nuit la Lune
   Sus les moindres flambeaus.
E bien qu'el soit an tel nombre si bele,
La beauté ét le moins qui soit en ele :
   Car le savoer qu'ele à,
E le parler qui soevemant distile,
Si vivemant anime d'un dous stile,
   Sont trop plus que cela.
Sus donq, mes vers, louèz cete Louïse :
Soièz, ma plume, a la louer soumise,
   Puis qu'ele à merité,
Maugre le tans fuitif, d'étre menee
Dessus le vol de la Fame ampannee
   A l'immortalité.

But I have seen, above all others, one
Shining as in the night there shines the moon
   Above the candlelight.
And while her beauty is a thing most rare,
Beauty is, even so, the least in her.
   This is because her learning,
The pleasure of her gracious conversation,

So charming in its wit and animation,
    Mean more to the discerning.
Therefore, my verses, you must praise Louise,
And you, my pen, in praising strive to please,
    For she deserves to be
Borne high upon the flying wings of fame,
Over the onward-rushing course of time,
    To immortality.

There is one portrait of Louise Labé made by Wœiriot of Lyons in 1555, now in the Bibliothèque Nationale. The engraver has left a likeness which has been an affront, however, to the sensibilities of some commentators. There have even been attempts to soften the hard lines of the portrait to make it conform more literally to *"la face plus angélique qu'humaine"* in the description of the good Guillaume Paradin (1573). These efforts are unsatisfactory. However uncompromising the Wœiriot portrait may seem, it shows an incorrigibly merry face with a dimple in the chin, mocking, intelligent eyes, a high forehead, and fair hair escaping in abundant curls from the restraint of the conventional coif. But it is unlikely that any picture would do justice to a face which doubtless owed much of its charm to quick change of feeling.

The real portrait of Louise Labé is to be found in what she wrote. She emerges wholly feminine, generous, indiscreet, delightful in her sense of humour, proud of her reputation for beauty and accomplishments but humble where her affections are involved.

In the Dedicatory Epistle, addressed to the gifted

and high-born Clémence de Bourges, Louise Labé is
the woman of letters, taking her stand in the dispute
of the century on the place of women in society and in
the arts. The letter begins: "The time having come,
Mademoiselle, when the severe laws of men no longer
hinder women from applying themselves to sciences
and other learning, it seems to me that those who can
must use that honest liberty so much desired by our
sex formerly to learn these things and show the men
what wrong they did us in depriving us of the advan-
tage and profit which might thus be ours. And if one
of us reaches the point where she can put her ideas
into writing, she should do so with care and should
not scorn the glory." She goes on to say, "the honour
that knowledge will procure for us will be entirely
ours, something that cannot be taken from us by the
cunning of thieves nor the strength of enemies nor the
lapse of time." And she invites the ladies of the city
to "lift their minds somewhat above the spindle and
the distaff for a while," maintaining that women in so
doing "will have rendered a public service in that men
will take more trouble and put more time on the study
of things cultural for fear of being put to shame by
seeing themselves outshone by those towards whom
they have always assumed an attitude of superiority
in everything."

In the *Débat de Folie et d'Amour*, Louise Labé is
the woman of the world. Here she presents a discus-
sion on love in the form of a play, the action taking
place in the Palace of Jupiter. The argument is merry
and wise. In an age when the manner of most prose

writers was heavy and monotonous, the style is easy, natural, and light. The expression is chaste and in marked contrast in this respect to the coarseness of contemporary story writers, not excepting the mystic Queen of Navarre. The characters—Jupiter, Venus, Apollo, Mercury, Folly, Love—are well defined. There is astonishing evidence of wide reading. This *Débat* was well known. It was translated into English in 1584—*The Debate between Love and Folly, translated out of the French by Robert Greene, Maister of Arts.*

The elegies ask for a sympathetic reading of the other poems, which are the twenty-four sonnets to follow, and of the love which inspired them. The second is a letter to her absent lover. In all three there is a plea for understanding.

The sonnets tell the story of Louise Labé in love. A number of them are undoubtedly among the earliest in the French language. They show a close acquaintance with the sonnets of Petrarch, for whom she acknowledges admiration. But there is none of the slavish imitation common to her day. While she makes use of the conventional devices of antithesis and of names borrowed from mythology, the song is her own. There was nothing devious in the language of her heart. The French critic, Emile Faguet, has called her sonnets *"les plus beaux vers passionés du monde."* Their beauty lies in their simplicity and sincerity. They are as intimately expressive as the music of her lute. There are spirited moments of audacity and humour but more often the record is of loneliness and disappointment.

If some of the sonnets are, as she says, the "foolish error of youth," others tell unmistakably the story of her love for the poet Olivier de Magny who came to Lyons on his way to Rome when Louise Labé was probably in her thirty-fifth year, the year before the publication of her work and of the Wœiriot portrait. It is known that Olivier de Magny loved her ardently and at first despairingly. Separation was cruel to him as well as to her in the weeks following his departure from Lyons, as shown by verses written to his friends. But by his own account Olivier de Magny was inclined to favour diversity in matters of the heart, and Rome had charms.

If Louise Labé wrote poetry after 1555, if the beauty and peace of the view from the terrace at her home in Parcieu inspired her to songs for her lute, nothing of these verses has survived.

But the personality of the woman has survived triumphantly. She was so vivid in her life that people in Lyons speak of her to-day as of someone still belonging. There are those who say, "O, Louise! . . ." hesitating as if to add, "Everyone knows about Louise, of course, but after all . . ." There is a note of regret, of excuse, of understanding. Others insist, even with indignation, that many things have been said about her which are not true. *"Elle a été beaucoup calomniée, vous savez!"* The city of Lyons has a warm memory of *La Belle Cordière;* and the street still bears her name.

A. L. C.

Lyon, France
July, 1949

For further information about Louise Labé the reader is referred to: *Louise Labé, sa vie et son œuvre* by Dorothy O'Connor (Paris, 1926), and to an article, *Louise Labé et sa famille,* by Georges Tricou, in *Humanisme et Renaissance* (1944).

LOUISE LABÉ (at thirty-five years of age).

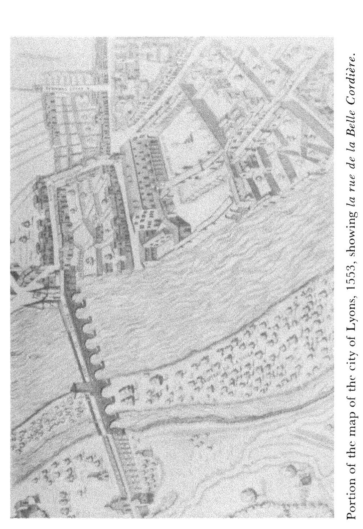

Portion of the map of the city of Lyons, 1553, showing *la rue de la Belle Cordière*.

An engraving of La Grange Blanche in the seventeenth century (as viewed from the court). At that time the building had been very little altered. Photograph supplied by M. Chalandon, the present owner of the property.

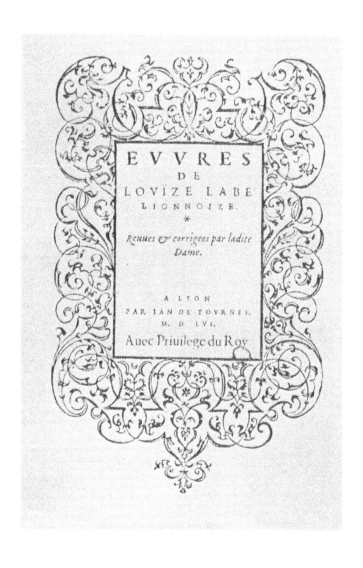

TITLE-PAGE, edition of 1556.

THE SONNETS

I

Non hauria Ulysse o qualunqu'altro mai
Piu accorto fù, da quel divino aspetto
Pien die gratie, d'honor & di rispetto
Sperato qual i sento affanni e guai.

Pur, Amor, co i begli ochi tu fatt' hai
Tal piaga dentro al mio innocente petto,
Di cibo & di calor gia tuo ricetto
Che rimedio non v'e si tu no'l dai.

O sorte dura, che mi fa esser quale
Punta d' un Scorpio, & domandar riparo
Contr' el velen' dall' istesso animale.

Chieggio li sol' ancida questa noia,
Non estingua el desir a me si caro,
Che mancar non potra ch' i non mi muoia.

I

No wisdom of Ulysses could foresee
The woe and the disquiet that are mine
From looking on that countenance divine,
So full of honour, charm, and dignity.

Two radiant eyes have hurt me grievously,
Wounding my heart. And, Love, the fault is thine;
While thou, the fountain of heart's warmth and wine,
Alone can furnish it the remedy.

O cruel fate that from a Scorpion sting
Requires that I must suffer, and entreat
The animal an antidote to bring!

End this my torment, but extinguish not
The need of love in me, that is so sweet
I could no longer live with love forgot.

O beaus yeus bruns, ô regars destournez,
O chaus soupirs, ô larmes espandues,
O noires nuits vainement atendues,
O jours luisans vainement retournez :

O tristes pleins, ô desirs obstinez
O tems perdu, ô peines despendues,
O mile morts en mile rets tendues,
O pires maus contre moy destinez.

O ris, ô front, cheveus, bras, mains & doits :
O lut pleintif, viole, archet & vois :
Tant de flambeaus pour ardre une femmelle !

De toy me plein, que tant de feus portant,
En tant d'endrois d'iceus mon cœur tatant,
N'en est sur toy volé quelque estincelle.

O dark and lovely eyes, O heedless gaze,
O burning sighs, O tears that fall as rain,
O sombre nights awaited all in vain,
O vain return of sun and shining days:

O obstinate desires, O moaning lays,
O wasted time, extravagance of pain,
O deaths that in a thousand traps have lain,
O darker destinies that haunt my ways.

O laugh, O brow, and locks, arms, hands, and fingers:
O sighing lute and viol, song that lingers:
Torches to fire the woman's heart in me!

But when so many firebrands thou dost bear
To set my heart ablaze, it is unfair
That never any spark should fall on thee.

III

O longs desirs, ô esperances vaines,
Tristes soupirs & larmes coutumieres
A engendrer de moy maintes rivieres,
Dont mes deus yeus sont sources & fontaines :

O cruautez, ô durtez inhumaines,
Piteus regars des celestes lumieres :
Du cœur transi ô passions premieres,
Estimez vous croitre encore mes peines ?

Qu'encor Amour sur moy son arc essaie,
Que nouveaus feus me gette et nouveaus dars :
Qu'il se despite, & pis qu'il pourra face :

Car je suis tant navree en toutes pars,
Que plus en moy une nouvelle plaie,
Pour m'empirer ne pourroit trouver place.

O longing, hope that empty solace brings,
Sighing and tears that from long habit rise
In many rivers from me, for mine eyes
Are but the fountains of them and the springs:

O cruel, O unkind my sufferings,
Pitiful, watching lanterns of the skies:
Can you, O passions of my youth, surprise
Pain in a heart where life no longer sings?

Let Love now train his bow on me again,
Let him pursue me with new fires, new darts,
In fury wreak more havoc than before:

Now am I wounded in so many parts,
No longer is there room for other pain
To find a place to hurt me any more.

IV

Depuis qu'Amour cruel empoisonna
Premierement de son feu ma poitrine,
Tousjours brulay de sa fureur divine,
Qui un seul jour mon cœur n'abandonna.

Quelque travail, dont assez me donna,
Quelque menasse & procheine ruïne :
Quelque penser de mort qui tout termine,
De rien mon cœur ardent ne s'estonna.

Tant plus qu'Amour nous vient fort assaillir,
Plus il nous fait nos forces recueillir,
Et tousjours frais en ses combats fait estre :

Mais ce n'est pas qu'en rien nous favorise,
Cil qui les Dieus et les hommes mesprise :
Mais pour plus fort contre les fors paroitre.

Since Love first laid his poison cruelly
Deep in my very being, fire and flame,
Divinely, madly, it has burned the same
And always, never once forsaking me.

Whatever pain, and pain there was to be,
Whatever threat of ruin or of blame,
Whatever thought of death, the end of fame,
Nothing could daunt my heart's audacity.

The longer his assault and the more cruel,
The more Love fortifies us for the duel,
For each affray he lends new energy;

But he who mocks at gods and mocks at men
Is showing us no hint of favour then:
Strength in a foe contents his vanity.

V

Clere Venus, qui erres par les Cieus,
Entens ma voix qui en pleins chantera,
Tant que ta face au haut du Ciel luira,
Son long travail & souci ennuieus.

Mon œil veillant s'atendrira bien mieus,
Et plus de pleurs te voyant gettera
Mieus mon lit mol de larmes baignera,
De ses travaux voyant témoins tes yeus.

Donq des humains sont les lassez esprits
De dous repos & de sommeil espris.
J'endure mal tant que le Soleil luit :

Et quand je suis quasi toute cassee,
Et que me suis mise en mon lit lassee,
Crier me faut mon mal toute la nuit.

V

Clear Venus, roaming in the heavenly plain,
Hear thou my voice that sorrowing shall rise
While yet thy radiance lingers in the skies,
To sing my desolation and my pain.

More quickly shall the tears collect again,
More plentifully drop from wakeful eyes,
When thou art witness of their enterprise,
And hotter shall they on my pillow rain.

So doth the heavy heart in human breast
Fall into love with sleep and gentle rest.
The hours are torment when the sun is bright;

And, worn to breaking when the day is past,
I lay me, weary, on my bed at last,
To cry my heartbreak through the lonely night.

Deus ou trois fois bienheureus le retour
De ce cler Astre, & plus heureus encore
Ce que son œil de regarder honore.
Que celle là recevroit un bon jour,

Qu'elle pourroit se vanter d'un bon tour
Qui baiseroit le plus beau don de Flore,
Le mieus sentant que jamais vid Aurore,
Et y feroit sur ses levres sejour !

C'est à moy seule à qui ce bien est du,
Pour tant de pleurs & tant de tems perdu :
Mais le voyant, tant lui feray de feste,

Tant emploiray de mes yeux le pouvoir,
Pour dessus lui plus de credit avoir,
Qu'en peu de temps feray grande conqueste.

Twice, three times blesséd that clear Star's return,
More blesséd still whatever shall invite
His radiant glance and waken to his light.
What gladness would she gather from the morn,

How proudly would she boast of Fortune's turn
Who kissed Aurora's darling, sweet delight,
And loveliest gift of Flora, gained the right
To find his lips and there to make sojourn!

For me alone this happiness is meant,
In recompense of time and tears misspent.
But I shall play him such a lovely tune,

So well employ the magic of a glance,
My influence and credit to enhance,
That I shall make a conquest very soon.

VII

On voit mourir toute chose animee,
Lors que du corps l'ame sutile part :
Je suis le corps, toy la meilleure part :
Ou es tu donq, ô ame bien aymee ?

Ne me laissez par si long temps pámee,
Pour me sauver apres viendrois trop tard.
Las, ne mets point ton corps en ce hazart :
Rens lui sa part & moitié estimee.

Mais fais, Ami, que ne soit dangereuse
Cette rencontre & revuë amoureuse,
L'acompagnant, non de severité,

Non de rigueur : mais de grace amiable,
Qui doucement me rende ta beaute,
Jadis cruelle, à present favorable.

We see the death of every living thing,
When soul from body leaves in subtle flight:
I am the body, thou, my soul, the light,
The better part. Where art thou loitering?

Leave me not fainting here so long. O bring
Me help before the swift approach of night.
Thy body pines; be mindful of its plight;
Restore the half it loves from wandering.

But see, dear one, that it be gently done,
In love encounters risk is often run.
No rigour must there be nor hint of duty,

But gracious charity will show thee how
In gentleness, to render me thy beauty,
A beauty cruel once but kinder now.

VIII

Je vis, je meurs : je me brule & me noye.
J'ay chaut estreme en endurant froidure :
La vie m'est & trop molle & trop dure.
J'ay grans ennuis entremeslez de joye :

Tout à un coup je ris & je larmoye,
Et en plaisir maint grief tourment j'endure :
Mon bien s'en va, & à jamais il dure :
Tout en un coup je seiche & je verdoye.

Ainsi Amour inconstamment me meine :
Et quand je pense avoir plus de douleur,
Sans y penser je me treuve hors de peine.

Puis quand je croy ma joye estre certeine,
Et estre au haut de mon desiré heur,
Il me remet en mon premier malheur.

I live, I die; I am on fire and drown;
I freeze while I am fainting from the heat;
Life is too bitter for me and too sweet:
And all my heavy care with joy is sown.

Out of my very laughter tears are born,
My pain is pleasure: happiness is fleet,
But dreams remain when present joys retreat:
I blossom when I am of bloom forlorn.

And so inconstantly Love leads me on:
When suffering seems more than I can bear,
I find, to my surprise, that pain has gone.

Then when I think it certain I have won
The only happiness for which I care,
He throws me back into my first despair.

Tout aussi tot que je commence à prendre
Dens le mol lit le repos desiré,
Mon triste esprit hors de moy retiré
S'en va vers toy incontinent se rendre.

Lors m'est avis que dedens mon sein tendre
Je tiens le bien, ou j'ay tant aspiré,
Et pour lequel j'ay si haut souspire,
Que de sanglots ay souvent cuidé fendre.

O dous sommeil, ô nuit à moy heureuse !
Plaisant repos, plein de tranquilité,
Continuez toutes les nuiz mon songe :

Et si jamais ma povre ame amoureuse
Ne doit avoir de bien en verité,
Faites au moins qu'elle en ait en mensonge.

No sooner do I seek a longed-for rest
Upon my bed than, swift withdrawn from me,
My sad and wayward spirit wilfully
Goes forth to meet thee in impatient quest.

Then do I seem to hold within my breast
Reward of longing, such felicity
As I have sighed for, until frequently,
Sobbing, I thought, would break a heart distressed.

O gentle, kindly sleep, O happy night!
O pleasant, sweet repose, and peaceful, still,
Continue every night to bring my dreaming:

Where lonely heart, and loving, never might
In very truth its happiness fulfil,
You bring of happiness at least the seeming.

Quand j'aperçoy ton blond chef couronné
D'un laurier verd, faire un Lut si bien pleindre
Que tu pourrois à te suivre contreindre
Arbres & rocs : quand je te vois orné,

Et de vertus dix mile environné,
Au chef d'honneur plus haut que nul ateindre :
Et des plus hauts les louenges esteindre :
Lors dit mon cœur en soy passionné :

Tant de vertus qui te font estre aymé,
Qui de chacun te font estre estimé,
Ne te pourroient aussi bien faire aymer ?

Et ajoutant à ta vertu louable
Ce nom encor de m'estre pitoyable,
De mon amour doucement t'enflamer ?

X

When thy fair head I see with laurel wound,
And when thy lute so plaintively doth play
That to thy service almost it would sway
The trees and rocks; when thus I see thee crowned,

And with ten thousand virtues decked around,
Attaining highest honours of thy day,
And from the highest taking praise away,
Then doth my heart a deep entreaty sound:

Those qualities that bring thee meed of fame,
From everyone affection and acclaim,
Could they, perhaps, thy heart to love incline?

Adding unto the gifts we praise in thee
The name of being merciful to me,
Take from my love a flame to kindle thine?

O dous regars, ô yeus pleins de beauté,
Petis jardins, pleins de fleurs amoureuses
Ou sont d'Amour les flesches dangereuses,
Tant à vous voir mon œil s'est arresté !

O cœur felon, ô rude cruauté,
Tant tu me tiens de façons rigoureuses,
Tant j'ay coulé de larmes langoureuses,
Sentant l'ardeur de mon cœur tourmenté !

Donques, mes yeus, tant de plaisir avez,
Tant de bons tours par ses yeus recevez :
Mais toy, mon cœur, plus les vois s'y complaire,

Plus tu languiz, plus en as de souci,
Or devinez si je suis aise aussi,
Sentant mon œil estre à mon cœur contraire.

Small gardens filled with beauty, gentle eyes
With tender flowers filled, where lurk the darts
Of Cupid, dangerous to mortal hearts,
So long my glance in wonder on thee lies!

O felon heart that charity denies,
So pitiless the practice of thine arts,
The ardour of a heart tormented starts
A flood of longing tears to sympathize!

And so, mine eyes, 'tis you that have the pleasure
From his receiving such reward of treasure;
While you, my heart, the more they are delighted,

The more you languish in anxiety,
And I cannot be satisfied, you see,
With heart and eyes of me so disunited.

XII

Lut, compagnon de ma calamité,
De mes soupirs témoin irreprochable,
De mes ennuis controlleur veritable,
Tu as souvent avec moy lamenté :

Et tant le pleur piteus t'a molesté,
Que commençant quelque son delectable,
Tu le rendois tout soudein lamentable,
Feignant le ton que plein avoit chanté.

Et si te veus efforcer au contraire,
Tu te destens & si me contreins taire :
Mais me voyant tendrement soupirer,

Donnant faveur à ma tant triste pleinte :
En mes ennuis me plaire suis contreinte,
Et d'un dous mal douce fin esperer.

Lute, my companion in calamity,
A faithful witness to my tears and sighing,
True record of unhappiness supplying,
Thou hast lamented oftentimes with me;

And so much hath my weeping piteously
Distressed thee that, some lovely song designing,
Thou hast refashioned it to a repining,
In sudden haste, to sing in company.

And when I would divert thee from thy will,
Thy silence doth constrain me to be still;
But watching me a-sighing here again,

From my so heavy grieving must thou borrow,
Until I find a beauty in my sorrow,
And hope for a sweet end to a sweet pain.

XIII

Oh si j'estois en ce beau sein ravie
De celui là pour lequel vois mourant :
Si avec lui vivre le demeurant
De mes cours jours ne m'empeschoit envie :

Si m'acollant me disoit, chere Amie,
Contentons nous l'un l'autre, s'asseurant
Que ja tempeste, Euripe, ne Courant
Ne nous pourra desjoindre en notre vie :

Si de mes bras le tenant acollé
Comme du Lierre est l'arbre encercelé,
La mort venoit, de mon aise envieuse :

Lors que souef plus il me baiseroit,
Et mon esprit sur ses levres fuiroit,
Bien je mourrois, plus que vivante, heureuse.

XIII

If only I might lie upon the breast
Of him for whom I think that I must die
Because of loving; if I could deny
The sweet desire to live with him the rest

Of my short days; if to his heart he pressed
Me saying, Dear one, you and I
River and tide and tempest can defy
To part us; let us love then undistressed:

If in my arms I held him close to me,
Binding him fast as ivy binds the tree,
And Death approached with envious caress,

While tenderly my love was kissing me,
Then if my spirit on his lips should flee,
Death would be life fulfilled in happiness.

Tant que mes yeus pourront larmes espandre,
A l'heur passé avec toy regretter :
Et qu'aus sanglots & soupirs resister
Pourra ma voix, & un peu faire entendre :

Tant que ma main pourra les cordes tendre
Du mignart Lut, pour tes graces chanter :
Tant que l'esprit se voudra contenter
De ne vouloir rien fors que toy comprendre :

Je ne souhaitte encore point mourir.
Mais quand mes yeus je sentiray tarir,
Ma voix cassee, & ma main impuissante,

Et mon esprit en ce mortel sejour
Ne pouvant plus montrer signe d'amante :
Priray la Mort noircir mon plus cler jour.

As long as I can weep remembering
The happiness of other days with thee,
And sighs and sobbing still may leave to me
My voice, and someone hears me when I sing;

As long as hand upon my lute can bring
Sweet music forth to praise thy quality,
As long as this my spirit still may be
Content in thee alone for everything;

So long I never shall desire to die:
But when I feel mine eyes begin to dry,
My voice unsure and impotent my hand,

My spirit, weary in captivity,
Without a sign of love at its command—
Come Death, cast down thy Shadow over me.

XV

Pour le retour du Soleil honorer,
Le Zephir, l'air serein lui apareille :
Et du sommeil l'eau & la terre esveille,
Qui les gardoit l'une de murmurer

En dous coulant, l'autre de se parer
De mainte fleur de couleur nompareille.
Ja les oiseaus es arbres font merveille,
Et aux passans font l'ennui moderer :

Les Nynfes ja en mile jeus s'esbatent
Au cler de Lune, & dansans l'herbe abatent :
Veus tu Zephir de ton heur me donner,

Et que par toy toute me renouvelle ?
Fay mon Soleil devers moy retourner,
Et tu verras s'il ne me rend plus belle.

XV

To honour the returning of the Sun,
Lo, the West Wind comes softly to arouse
The silent waters and the earth that drowse,
Until the rippling murmur of the one

Is heard, and flowers without comparison
In beauty deck the other. From the boughs
Already joyous carolling endows
The passer-by with joy, and care is done;

Already nymphs at play are nightly seen
By moonlight, dancing on the trodden green.
Give me, sweet wind, of thy serenity,

Thereby all things about me to renew;
Constrain my Sun to turn again to me
And see how he shall make me lovelier too.

Apres qu'un tems la gresle & le tonnerre
Ont le haut mont de Caucase batu,
Le beau jour vient, de lueur revétu.
Quand Phebus ha son cerne fait en terre,

Et l'Ocean il regaigne à grand erre :
Sa seur se montre avec son chef pointu.
Quand quelque tems le Parthe ha combatu,
Il prent la fuite & son arc il desserre.

Un tems t'ay vù & consolé pleintif,
Et defiant de mon feu peu hatif :
Mais maintenant que tu m'as embrasee,

Et suis au point auquel tu me voulois,
Tu as to flame en quelque eau arrosee
Et es plus froit qu'estre je ne soulois.

When thunder in the Caucasus and sleet
Have beat upon the mountains all the night,
Then comes the lovely dawn arrayed in light.
When Phoebus with his earthly span complete

Rides swiftly down into his Ocean seat,
His sister's pointed head comes into sight.
The Parthian after labour in the fight
Flees and lets fly his arrow in retreat.

Once have I known thee beg to be consoled,
Mistrustful of a fire too well controlled;
Now thou hast kindled me, now thou dost know

That I am where thou long hast wanted me,
Thy flame is dampened, perished is its glow,
Colder thou art than I was wont to be.

XVII

Je fuis la vile, & temples, & tous lieus,
Esquels prenant plaisir à t'ouir pleindre,
Tu peus, & non sans force, me contreindre
De te donner ce qu'estimois le mieus.

Masques, tournois, jeus me sont ennuieus,
Et rien sans toy de beau ne me puis peindre :
Tant que tâchant à ce desir esteindre,
Et un nouvel obget faire à mes yeus,

Et des pensers amoureus me distraire,
Des bois espais sui le plus solitaire :
Mais j'aperçoy, ayant erré maint tour,

Que si je veus de toy estre delivre
Il me convient hors de moymesme vivre,
Ou fais encor que loin sois en sejour.

I flee the town, its temples, everywhere
Enchanted with thy pleading, for I know
Thou couldst prevail upon me to bestow
On thee, perforce, all that I deemed most rare.

I cannot picture anything as fair
Without thee: masking, games are empty show;
Till striving this my longing to outgrow,
To find some other thing for which to care,

To be distracted from these love thoughts only,
Through deepest woods I take the path most lonely,
But having wandered endlessly, I see

That if I would be free, for this conversion,
I must be someone else, some other person,
Or dwell a thousand miles away from thee.

XVIII

Baise m'encor, rebaise moy & baise :
Donne m'en un de tes plus savoureus,
Donne m'en un de tes plus amoureus :
Je t'en rendray quatre plus chaus que braise.

Las, te pleins tu ? ça que ce mal j'apaise,
En t'en donnant dix autres doucereus.
Ainsi meslans nos baisers tant heureus
Jouissons nous l'un de l'autre à notre aise.

Lors double vie à chacun en suivra.
Chacun en soy & son ami vivra.
Permets m'Amour penser quelque folie :

Tousjours suis mal, vivant discrettement,
Et ne me puis donner contentement,
Si hors de moy ne fay quelque saillie.

XVIII

Kiss me again, again, and then once more:
Give me one of the sweetest thou canst find,
And now another one for love designed.
Hotter than living coals I give back four;

They hurt, alas! For healing let me pour
The balm of ten more, gentle ones and kind.
So let us mingle kisses, let us bind
Our love with happy kisses, and adore.

Loving is living twice, so for each one
Life will be in each other and alone.
Allow me, Love, invention of this folly,

I suffer always when I live discreetly,
Contentment never can I find completely
Unless, betimes, I make some foolish sally.

Diane estant en l'espesseur d'un bois,
Apres avoir mainte beste assenee,
Prenoit le frais, de Nynfes couronnee :
J'allois resvant comme fay maintefois,

Sans y penser : quand j'ouy une vois
Qui m'apela, disant, Nynfe estonnee,
Que ne t'es tu vers Diane tournee ?
Et me voyant sans arc & sans carquois,

Qu'as-tu trouvé, ô compagne, en ta voye
Qui de ton arc & flesches ait fait proye ?
Je m'animay, respons je, à un passant,

Et lui getay en vain toutes mes flesches
Et l'arc apres : mais lui les ramassant
Et les tirant me fit cent & cent bresches.

Diana, having found a welcome shade
In ancient woods, the day's fierce hunting done,
Crowned by her nymphs took refuge from the sun;
And dreaming as I often do, I strayed

In careless fashion, then perforce obeyed
The voice that called me, saying, wherefore shun
Diana, startled nymph, and who hath won
Quiver and bow from thee? Art thou afraid

To tell me who it was, upon the way,
Took bow and arrows from thee for his prey?
A stranger passing troubled me, I sighed,

And all my arrows did I cast in vain,
My bow as well. He took them and replied
By wounding me again and yet again.

XX

Predit me fut, que devois fermement
Un jour aymer celui dont la figure
Me fut descrite : & sans autre peinture
Le reconnu quand vy premierement :

Puis le voyant aymer fatalement
Pitié je pris de sa triste aventure :
Et tellement je forcay ma nature,
Qu'autant que lui aymay ardentement.

Qui n'ust pensé qu'en faveur devoit croitre
Ce que le Ciel & destins firent naitre ?
Mais quand je voy si nubileus aprets,

Vents si cruels & tant horrible orage :
Je croy qu'estoient les infernaus arrets
Qui de si loin m'ourdissoient ce naufrage.

XX

It was foretold I should adore one day
The one whose features were described to me,
And with no other picture, instantly
I recognized him when he crossed my way.

Then, seeing him of Love the sorry prey,
I took compassion on his misery
And forced my nature into sympathy,
Till love as ardent did my heart betray.

Incredible that what was Heaven born
Should thus of growth and favour be forlorn,
But when this darkening of clouds I see,

This horror of the storm and winds in strife,
I think that Hell hath fashioned the decree
That from afar made shipwreck of my life.

Quelle grandeur rend l'homme venerable ?
Quelle grosseur ? Quel poil ? quelle couleur ?
Qui est des yeus le plus emmieleur ?
Qui fait plus tot une playe incurable ?

Quel chant est plus à l'homme convenable ?
Qui plus penetre en chantant sa douleur ?
Qui un dous lut fait encore meilleur ?
Quel naturel est le plus amiable ?

Je ne voudrois le dire assurément
Ayant Amour forcé mon jugement :
Mais je say bien & de tant je m'assure,

Que tout le beau que l'on pourroit choisir,
Et que tout l'art qui ayde la Nature,
Ne me sauroient acroitre mon desir.

What stature in a man doth breed respect?
What size? And what complexion, dark or fair?
Who hath the eyes to flatter and ensnare?
And what can soonest wound with sure effect?

What song and story should a man select?
Whose singing penetrates in its despair?
And on his lute who plays the sweetest air?
What nature in a man should one elect?

I would not answer you assuredly,
For Love creates a prejudice in me;
But well I know and this I tell you true,

No beauty anywhere nor subtle art
Adorning Nature's loveliness anew,
Could strengthen the desire within my heart.

Luisant Soleil, que tu es bien heureus,
De voir tousjours de t'Amie la face :
Et toy, sa seur, qu'Endimion embrasse,
Tant te repais de miel amoureus.

Mars voit Venus : Mercure aventureus
De Ciel en Ciel, de lieu en lieu se glasse :
Et Jupiter remarque en mainte place
Ses premiers ans plus gays & chaleureus.

Voilà du Ciel la puissante harmonie,
Qui les esprits divins ensemble lie :
Mais s'ils avoient ce qu'ils ayment lointein,

Leur harmonie & ordre irrevocable
Se tourneroit en erreur variable,
Et comme moy travailleroient en vain.

How fortunate thou art, O shining Sun,
Of thy Beloved to regard the face,
And thou, his sister, rich in the embrace
Of thy sweet lover, thy Endymion.

Mars looks on Venus, Mercury doth run
From sky to sky, adventure in his race,
And Jupiter observes in many a place
Gay records of the years forever gone.

Behold the powerful harmony that binds
Together in the sky celestial minds.
But should the object of their love be ta'en,

The constant order and the harmony
Would turn to discord and inconstancy,
Like me they would know torment, and in vain.

XXIII

Las ! que me sert, que si parfaitement
Louas jadis & ma tresse doree,
Et de mes yeus la beauté comparee
A deux Soleils, dont Amour finement

Tira les trets causez de ton tourment ?
Ou estes vous, pleurs de peu de duree ?
Et Mort par qui devoit estre honoree
Ta ferme amour & iteré serment ?

Donques c'estoit le but de la malice
De m'asservir sous ombre de service ?
Pardonne moy, Ami, à cette fois,

Estant outree & de despit & d'ire :
Mais je m'assure, quelque part que tu sois,
Qu'autant que moy tu soufres de martire.

Alas! What doth it serve that perfectly
Thou hast sung praises to my golden hair,
That beauty of mine eyes thou shouldst compare
To Suns whence Love with cunning artistry

Hath drawn the darts that caused thine agony?
Where are the tears of that so brief despair?
And laggard death that was to be the fair
Crown of thy love and sworn fidelity?

Thy homage, then, was but a cloak to hide
Ambition to annihilate my pride!
Forgive me, dear; my over-burdened heart

In bitterness and anger speaks for me;
In truth I am assured, where'er thou art,
Thy martyrdom is great as mine can be.

XXIV

Ne reprenez, Dames, si j'ay aymé :
Si j'ay senti mile torches ardantes,
Mile travaus, mile douleurs mordantes :
Si en pleurant, j'ay mon tems consumé,

Las que mon nom n'en soit par vous blamé.
Si j'ay failli, les peines sont presentes,
N'aigrissez point leurs pointes violentes :
Mais estimez qu'Amour, à point nommé,

Sans votre ardeur d'un Vulcan excuser
Sans la beauté d'Adonis acuser,
Pourra, s'il veut, plus vous rendre amoureuses :

En ayant moins que moi d'ocasion,
Et plus d'estrange & forte passion.
Et gardez vous d'estre plus malheureuses.

If I have loved, then, Ladies, do not chide,
If I have felt the flaming touch, the bane
Of love a thousand times, the biting pain,
If hours were wasted as I wept and sighed,

Alas, why should my name by you be tried?
If I have faltered, memories remain
To hurt me: wherefore sharpen them again?
Do not forget that Love may yet decide,

Without the fire of Vulcan to excuse,
Or beauty of Adonis to accuse,
To make a victim, even more, of you;

With less occasion than is mine, your passion
May act in stranger and in stronger fashion.
Beware of feeling more unhappy too.